Guided Ref

MW01194524

Praying
with Scripture

VOLUME 1

LOYOLAPRESS.
A JESUIT MINISTRY
Chicago

LOYOLA PRESS.
A JESUIT MINISTRY

3441 N. Ashland Avenue
Chicago, Illinois 60657
(800) 621-1008
www.loyolapress.com

Guided Reflection material adapted from *Finding God: Our Response to God's Gifts*
© 2005 Loyola Press, Chicago, Illinois.

The Scripture quotations contained herein are from the *New Revised Standard
Version Bible: Catholic Edition* copyright © 1993 and 1989 by the Division of
Christian Education of the National Council of the Churches of Christ in the U.S.A.
Used by permission. All rights reserved.

Cover illustration by Joy Allen
Cover design by Maggie Hong
Interior design by Mia McGloin and Maggie Hong

ISBN 13: 978-0-8294-2852-0
ISBN: 10: 0-8294-2852-6

Printed in the United States of America
08 09 10 11 12 Bang 10 9 8 7 6 5 4 3 2 1

Contents

How To Use This Book

This book contains 10 ready-to-use guided reflections, each based on a specific Scripture passage. The reflections are designed for use by catechists, teachers and parents of children in the elementary grades. Each reflection follows a simple, step-by-step format that will help both you and the children grow comfortable and confident in praying reflectively.

Getting Ready for Reflective Prayer

Prior to using these reflections with the children, you will want to spend sufficient time in preparation. Praying with the Scripture passage and reading the text of the reflection aloud several times will help you to be comfortable with the flow. You may find you need to adapt the text to meet the particular needs of your group, shorten or lengthen the pauses, or change the vocabulary. Establish a comfortable, quiet, and prayerful environment and mood to help the children let go of any distractions.

Consider the following as you prepare to lead the prayer:

Prayer Environment

It is always desirable to have a specific place for prayer, easily recognizable by its décor. A cloth, Bible, plant, and religious symbols such as a crucifix, an icon, or a holy picture are all useful to set the mood and help the children to focus their attention.

Prayer Postures

Developing a comfortable posture for reflective prayer is a useful habit. Help the children experiment with a variety of postures to find one in which they can be comfortable yet alert. Encourage them to close their eyes or to focus their attention on a symbol you have provided in the prayer environment. As children grow familiar with this style of prayer, they will move into their preferred posture right away.

Reflective Music

The use of well-chosen, quiet, instrumental music can enhance reflective prayer by providing a soothing setting for relaxation and by covering distractions. Look for music whose melody will not be recognizable to the children. This helps to avoid the possibility of lyrics coming to mind, thus distracting the children during the reflection.

Steps for Reflective Prayer

The following steps provide the prayer leader with valuable information and background for guiding the children in reflective prayer.

Set the Stage

In order to get the most from the Scripture message, help the children begin with their own experience. By using the questions provided or ones of your own, lead the children in a sharing of life experiences that relate to some aspect of the Scripture reading. Be sure to keep the sharing brief.

Read the Scripture

After the time of sharing, link the children's experience to the Scripture they are about to hear. You can use the suggestion provided or create your own. Then read the Scripture passage. While the Scripture is included here for your convenience, it is always preferable to read directly from the Bible. A good children's or youth Bible will be an invaluable resource to have on hand.

Connect the Experience

This step helps the children connect their experience and the Scripture they just heard with the theme of the reflection. It gives a hint of what is to come and begins the transition into the actual time of reflection.

Prepare for Prayer

In this step the children get comfortable and begin to relax through deep breathing. [For tips on postures, see the section *Prayer Postures*.] Spending time in this step is invaluable to the rest of the reflection. Ask the children to rest their hands in their laps. You may want to do some practice breathing techniques prior to beginning the time of reflective prayer. Help the children establish a rhythm to their breathing. Count slowly to three as the children inhale. Tell them to hold their breath for a count of three, and then exhale as you count to three.

Lead the Meditation

Be sure to pray through the meditation yourself several times before leading the children in prayer. Practice reading slowly and clearly, and decide how long to pause at each indication. You will want to lengthen the pauses for older children and shorten them for younger ones. No matter the age group, allow sufficient time for the children to reflect and meet God in the silence of their hearts.

Conclude the Meditation

Once the reflection is over and the children have opened their eyes, engage them in a prayer or an appropriate song to bring closure to the time of prayer. It is important that you prepare this in advance and that the children are familiar with whatever you choose. A sung refrain, perhaps one used at Mass, with simple gestures can be a good way for the children to use their bodies and voices for prayer. Avoid discussion about their prayer time with Jesus. Allow it to be private, just between Jesus and the child. If someone really wants to talk, make time for him or her later. At the conclusion, use a few gentle words to make the transition from prayer time to your next activity.

An Additional Model: *The Ball of Red String*

The last two reflections in this volume are based on the popular Loyola Press prayer resource *The Ball of Red String* by Sr. Marlene Halpin, O.P. Through the use of their imaginations, the children will be guided to follow a ball of red string as it unravels, leading them to their Heart Home and a prayerful encounter with Jesus.

When using these reflections, you may want to prepare small balls of red yarn for each child to take away as a reminder of their prayer time and how to find Jesus in their hearts.

Let the Children Come ⤳

Set the Stage

Prepare the children to enter into prayer by helping them reflect on their own experiences. Ask some leading questions. Use the questions below or questions of your own.

- Have you ever been to an event where you were so far back you couldn't see? What was it like? What did you do?

- Has anyone ever told you that you were too young to do something you really wanted to do? How did you feel?

Read the Scripture

Prepare the children to hear the Scripture by linking their experience to the Scripture theme. Use these words or your own.

> Let's listen to a story from the Gospel of Mark. We'll hear about a time when some children were trying to get close to Jesus, but were prevented from doing so. When they were finally allowed to come near him, they received even more than they expected.

Mark 10:13–16

> People were bringing little children to him in order that he might touch them; and the disciples spoke sternly to them. But when Jesus saw this, he was indignant and said to them, "Let the little children come to me; do not stop them; for it is to such as these that the kingdom of God belongs. Truly I tell you, whoever does not receive the kingdom of God as a little child will never enter it." And he took them up in his arms, laid his hands on them, and blessed them.

Connect the Experience

Help the children connect their experience to the theme of the prayer. Use these words or your own.

> Today we are going to use our imaginations to travel back to the time of Jesus. As you make your way to the front of the crowd

that is gathered around him, think about what you would like to say to Jesus.

Prepare for Prayer

First, invite the children to make themselves as comfortable as they can. Next, lead them to grow quiet by focusing on their breath.

To enter into this time of prayer, we first need to make ourselves comfortable. Leave enough space around you so that nothing distracts you. *[Pause]* Close your eyes and let yourself grow still. *[Pause]* Now take a few moments to pay attention to your breath. *[Pause]* Can you feel your breath make your chest rise and fall? *[Pause]* Take a slow, deep breath in *[Pause]*, hold *[Pause]*, then slowly and silently exhale. *[Pause]* Again, take another slow, deep breath in *[Pause]*, hold *[Pause]*, and silently exhale. *[Pause, and repeat as necessary.]*

Lead the Meditation

Imagine that you are outside and you notice a large crowd of people. *[Pause]* As you hear people talking, you realize that they've come to listen to Jesus. How exciting! But the crowd is so huge that you can't see Jesus. There is no tree to climb and no wall to stand on. Listen closely. Can you hear Jesus at all? *[Pause]*

Carefully you start moving through the crowd toward Jesus' voice. You say, "Excuse me," "Pardon me," "I'm sorry," as you bump your way past all the people. Are you getting any closer to Jesus? *[Pause]* You keep moving toward the sound of Jesus' voice. Finally you find an opening in the crowd. Jesus is in the very middle of a large circle of people. There are dozens of adults and children around him. You stop to listen for a while. Do you stand or sit on the ground? Make yourself as comfortable as you can. Watch and listen as Jesus teaches the people. *[Pause]*

Grown-ups start bringing their children to meet Jesus. His friends, the apostles, notice this and become impatient. They say, "Don't bother Jesus with the children." When Jesus hears this, he becomes upset because he loves children. He smiles at them and says to the apostles and to everyone, "Bring the children to me. They are very special people." You watch as all of the children come forward. *[Pause]* Jesus hugs them, places his hands on their heads, and blesses them. Can you see how much Jesus loves the children? *[Pause]*

Now Jesus notices you. Maybe he winks and smiles at you. Do you wink back? Do you smile? Maybe wave? *[Pause]* Jesus keeps talking. Some of the grownups are asking him questions. Patiently he answers each one. After a while Jesus looks over to you again. This time he walks in your direction. *[Pause]* Standing before you, Jesus says your name and tells you that he's happy to see you. Even though there's a crowd of people, you feel like you and Jesus are alone. What do you say to Jesus? *[Pause]* Do you bring him up-to-date on what you're learning? Or perhaps you tell him what's going on with your friends. *[Pause]* Maybe there's something else you'd rather talk about with Jesus. *[Pause]*

Jesus listens and then he answers you. Listen to him with your heart. *[Pause]* Feel how much Jesus loves you. *[Long pause]* What does Jesus want you to know from him? *[Pause]* Maybe he has a question for you. If so, answer him thoughtfully. *[Pause]* Remember that Jesus loves you. You can always be sure of that. *[Pause]*

You're enjoying your visit with Jesus so much that you don't realize what time it is. The sun is lower in the sky, and the air is getting cooler. The crowd is much smaller now, and you realize that it's almost time for you to go. *[Pause]* Before you leave, Jesus asks you a question. He wants to know if you would like to go with him for a few minutes to be with God the Father. God loves your company. You know you never have to worry about talking with God. Sometimes you can use words. Other times it's enough simply to show God your mind and heart. God always understands what we mean, even without words. *[Pause]*

And now for the best part! You and Jesus sit quietly together, heart-to-heart with God the Father. *[Pause]* Let yourself be loved by God. *[Pause]* Feel the great love God has for you. *[Pause]* With an open heart, just rest in God's presence. *[Long pause]* If there is something you would like to share with God, do it now. You know God loves to hear from you. *[Pause]* Listen for anything God might have to share with you.

You sense it's time to be leaving. You say goodbye for now to God the Father and return with Jesus to where you met him. He gently puts his hand on your head and blesses you. *[Pause]* Jesus tells you how special you are to him and that you can visit with him anytime you'd like. He loves spending time with you. *[Pause]* You say thank you to Jesus. Do you say when you'll be back? Perhaps you don't quite know yet, and Jesus reminds you to spend time with him again soon. *[Pause]*

You and Jesus say goodbye for now. *[Pause]* As you leave, you think about how you felt when you were with Jesus. *[Pause]* You walk past the remaining people still gathered around Jesus and make your way back to this room. *[Pause]* When you are ready, open your eyes. *[Pause]* Stretch if you'd like. *[Pause]* Look around. We're all here. We're back together again.

Conclude the Meditation

Close the time of meditation with an appropriate prayer (for example, Glory Be to the Father) or a sung refrain (for example, Alleluia) that the children already know. You may wish to add easy-to-learn gestures.

In My Father's House ⤳

Set the Stage

Prepare the children to enter into prayer by helping them reflect on their own experiences. Ask some leading questions. Use the questions below or questions of your own.

- Have you ever been so involved in something that you lost track of time? What happened?

- Have you ever accidentally done something that caused your parents to worry about you? How did you feel afterward?

Read the Scripture

Prepare the children to hear the Scripture by linking their experience to the Scripture theme. Use these words or your own.

> Let's listen to a story from the Gospel of Luke. We'll hear about a time when the boy Jesus got so involved with the teachers in the Temple that he lost track of time and was separated from his parents for three days.

Luke 2:41–52

Now every year his parents went to Jerusalem for the festival of the Passover. And when he was twelve years old, they went up as usual for the festival. When the festival was ended and they started to return, the boy Jesus stayed behind in Jerusalem, but his parents did not know it. Assuming that he was in the group of travelers, they went a day's journey. Then they started to look for him among their relatives and friends. When they did not find him, they returned to Jerusalem to search for him. After three days they found him in the temple, sitting among the teachers, listening to them and asking them questions. And all who heard him were amazed at his understanding and his answers. When his parents saw him they were astonished; and his mother said to him, "Child, why have you treated us like this? Look, your father and I have been searching for you in great anxiety." He said to them, "Why were you searching for me? Did you not know that I must be in my Father's house?" But they did not understand what he said to them. Then he went down with them and came to Nazareth, and was obedient to them. His mother treasured all these things in her heart.

And Jesus increased in wisdom and in years, and in divine and human favor.

Connect the Experience

Help the children connect their experience to the theme of the prayer. Use these words or your own.

Today we're going to use our imaginations to meet the boy Jesus after this event took place. As you speak with him in prayer, remember that he had many experiences in his life that are similar to your own.

Prepare for Prayer

First, invite the children to make themselves as comfortable as they can. Next, lead them to grow quiet by focusing on their breath.

To enter into this time of prayer, we first need to make ourselves comfortable. Leave enough space around you so that nothing distracts you. [Pause] Now close your eyes and let yourself grow still. [Pause] Take a few moments to pay attention to your breath. [Pause] Can you feel your breath make your chest rise and fall? [Pause] Take a slow, deep breath in [Pause], hold [Pause], then slowly and silently exhale. [Pause] Again, take another slow, deep breath in [Pause], hold [Pause], and silently exhale. [Pause, and repeat as necessary]

Lead the Meditation

Do you know anybody in the seventh grade? Maybe you have a brother or a sister or a cousin there. If you don't, imagine a seventh grader you may have seen at school or in your neighborhood. [Pause] That's the age Jesus was when Mary and Joseph thought they lost him after the festival. He was almost a teenager, but he wasn't really grown up yet.

Now imagine that Jesus and his parents have moved into your neighborhood. That'll make it easy for you to meet him. In your imagination, you're sitting outside, waiting for your friends to come over. [Pause] Across the street, you notice a boy who looks about 12 years old. The boy smiles at you and walks over. *[Pause]* You can't believe your eyes! You recognize this 12-year old. It's Jesus! He calls to you and says hi. How do you feel when he notices you? *[Pause]* Perhaps Jesus sits down right next to you. Do you move over a little bit to make room? Then side by side, you sit and chat for a while. *[Pause]* Jesus is so friendly, it isn't hard to talk with him. And he's really interested in knowing all about you. *[Pause]*

Jesus is especially interested in what you've been learning. Well, there are so many things you learn each day, you can't tell him everything. But you do want to tell him some things. Choose which things you'd like to talk about. Take some time to tell him about that now. *[Pause]* Jesus smiles because he knows that you just heard the story of when he stayed back in the Temple after the festival, the time when Mary and Joseph couldn't find him. What did you notice most about the story? *[Pause]* Jesus is ready to talk about that. He remembers it very well. *[Pause]*

You can probably remember a time when you got so involved in something that you totally lost track of time. Perhaps it was something you're good at, or maybe it was something you care about deeply and requires concentration. What was it you were doing? *[Pause]* Were you supposed to be home at a certain time? Were your parents worried? Were they looking for you? *[Pause]* Jesus' experience is probably something like yours.

Listen for what Jesus wants you to remember about what happened after Mary and Joseph found him. What does he share with you? *[Pause]* Maybe Jesus goes on to tell you that he left Jerusalem and went home with his parents. And as he grew up, he obeyed them, respected them, and loved them. *[Pause]* Tell Jesus how it is with your parents. Let him know what it's like for you at home. *[Long pause]* Jesus nods as he listens. You can tell that he understands. *[Pause]* Now think of what you like best about being a child in your family and share that with Jesus. *[Pause]* If there's anything else you'd like to share with him, take a few moments to do that now. *[Pause]*

Then Jesus asks you a question. He wants to know if you would like to go with him for a few minutes to be with God the Father. God loves your company. You know you never have to worry about talking with God. God always understands what we mean whether we use words or not. The important thing is just to open your heart and mind to God. *[Pause]*

And now for the best part! You and Jesus sit quietly together, heart-to-heart with God our Father. *[Pause]* Let yourself be loved by God. *[Pause]* With an open heart, just rest in God's presence. *[Long pause]*

If there is something you would like to share with God, do it now. You know God loves to hear from you. *[Pause]* Listen for anything God might have to share with you. *[Pause]*

You sense it's time to be leaving. You say goodbye for now to God the Father and return with Jesus to your neighborhood. *[Pause]* You can tell how much Jesus loves you and likes spending time with you.

You and Jesus say goodbye for now. You thank him for this time together. *[Pause]* You know you can meet again whenever you'd like. You watch as Jesus walks away, waving to you as he crosses the street. *[Pause]*

Now slowly come back to the room. When you are ready, open your eyes. *[Pause]* Stretch your arms. *[Pause]* Silently look around. *[Pause]* Welcome back!

Conclude the Meditation

Close the time of meditation with an appropriate prayer (for example, Glory Be to the Father) or a sung refrain (for example, Alleluia) which the children already know. You may wish to add easy-to-learn gestures.

Yeast and Seeds ⤳

Set the Stage

Prepare the children to enter into prayer by helping them reflect on their own experiences. Ask some leading questions. Use the questions below or questions of your own.

- Have you ever planted seeds and then watched them grow? What did you notice?

- Have you ever watched someone make bread from scratch? Do you know what the special ingredient is?

Read the Scripture

Prepare the children to hear the Scripture by linking their experience to the Scripture theme. Use these words or your own.

> Today we're going to hear two stories from the Gospel of Matthew. One is about what happens to dough when you add yeast, and the other is about how big a tiny seed can grow. Jesus used these stories, called parables, to teach the people what the Kingdom of God is like.

Matthew 13:31–33

> He put before them another parable: "The kingdom of heaven is like a mustard seed that someone took and sowed in his field; it is the smallest of all the seeds, but when it has grown it is the greatest of shrubs and becomes a tree, so that the birds of the air come and make nests in its branches.

> He told them another parable: "The kingdom of heaven is like yeast that a woman took and mixed in with three measures of flour until all of it was leavened."

Connect the Experience

Help the children connect their experience to the theme of the prayer. Use these words or your own.

- Now, through the use of our imaginations, we're going to spend some time with Jesus. As you listen to Jesus teaching the people, think about ways that you are like yeast or a tiny seed.

Prepare for Prayer

First, invite the children to make themselves as comfortable as they can. Next, lead them to grow quiet by focusing on their breath.

To enter into this time of prayer, we first need to make ourselves comfortable. Leave enough space around you so that nothing distracts you. *[Pause]* Now close your eyes and let yourself grow still. *[Pause]* Take a few moments to pay attention to your breath. *[Pause]* Can you feel your breath make your chest rise and fall? *[Pause]* Take a slow, deep breath in *[Pause]*, hold *[Pause]*, then slowly and silently exhale. *[Pause]* Again, take another slow, deep breath in *[Pause]*, hold *[Pause]*, and silently exhale. *[Pause, and repeat as necessary]*

Lead the Meditation

In your imagination, picture a place where you'd like to be. Maybe you've been there before and would like to go back. Maybe it's some place you've read about or seen on TV. Maybe it's right in your own home. The important thing is that you like to be there. In your imagination, go to that place now. *[Pause]*

Someone is coming to join you. Look, it's Jesus! You are so glad to see each other. Do you greet him with a smile? How does he greet you? *[Pause]* Welcome him to your favorite place. You might want to tell him what you like about this place and show him around. Why don't you do it now? *[Pause]* Maybe Jesus asks how you are. How do you answer him? *[Pause]* Share with him what's going on at home and in school. Is there something special you want to talk about with him? Tell him now if you'd like. *[Pause]*

Jesus knows that you've just heard the parables of the mustard seed and the yeast. You tell him what you know about these stories. *[Pause]* Maybe you wonder why he teaches people with parables. If so, now's the time to ask him. *[Pause]* Jesus is likely to remind you that he speaks in parables because some things are so big, so wonderful, so precious that you can't talk about them exactly. The Kingdom of God is like that. *[Pause]*

To remind you of the parable of the mustard seed, Jesus holds out his fist and opens it. What do you think it is? *[Pause]* If you guessed a mustard seed, you're right! Jesus is holding the tiniest of seeds, a mustard seed. It's so small you have to look very carefully to see it. Touch the seed. *[Pause]* Does it stick to your finger? Notice how small it is compared to your finger. What do you think will happen if you plant this seed and tend it with care? Will the seed grow? *[Pause]* How long might it take? *[Pause]* How big can it get? *[Pause]* You remember that the mustard seed becomes a bush so large that birds can live in its branches.

Jesus is glad you like this story. Next, he reminds you that this tiny mustard seed is like the Kingdom of God. A seed and a kingdom? Hmm. Jesus can see you're beginning to catch on now. You remind Jesus about the parable of the yeast. Jesus has a big smile for that one. And so he asks you what you know about it. Tell him what a little bit of yeast does. *[Pause]* Did you tell him how powerful that little bit of yeast is, that it touches every particle of the dough to make the bread rise? *[Pause]*

Now for the hard part. If Jesus asks you what these parables about the Kingdom of God mean to you, what will you say? *[Pause]* Maybe you tell him that you can be like the mustard seed, doing small things that are a big help to others. *[Pause]* What are some of these things you can do? Talk it over with Jesus and see what he thinks. *[Pause]*

Jesus smiles warmly and you can tell that he has more questions. How do you make life better for other people? What do you do? How are you that little bit of yeast in your family, at school, and with your friends? What can you think of? Share it with Jesus now. *[Pause]*

Jesus smiles. He asks you ever so gently if you are willing to keep doing little kindnesses and good deeds, and wait patiently to grow. Are you? How do you answer him? *[Pause]* Why not ask Jesus to help you find ways to be a tiny seed or a little bit of yeast so that his Kingdom comes? Spend a minute with Jesus, listening for what he might tell you. *[Pause]* Feel how much he loves you. *[Pause]*

Now Jesus asks you another question. He wants to know if you would like to go with him for a few minutes to be with God the Father. God loves spending time with you no matter where you are. *[Pause]*

And now for the best part! You and Jesus sit quietly together, heart-to-heart with God our Father. *[Pause]* Let yourself be loved by God. *[Pause]* With an open heart, just rest in God's presence. *[Long pause]* If there is something you would like to share with

God, do it now. You know God loves to hear from you. *[Pause]* Listen for anything God might have to share with you. *[Pause]*

You sense it will soon be time to leave. You say goodbye for now to God the Father and return with Jesus to your favorite place. *[Pause]* Now, knowing that you'll be leaving soon, Jesus puts the tiny mustard seed in your hand. He invites you to plant it and tend it and watch it grow. *[Pause]* You thank Jesus for the seed and for his parables. But before you leave, spend a moment telling Jesus about anything else that's on your mind. *[Pause]*

Jesus promises to always be there to help you. With this promise in mind, you say goodbye to Jesus, knowing that you'll see him again very soon. *[Pause]* Now gradually bring yourself back to this room. *[Pause]* Open your eyes. *[Pause]* Stretch if you'd like. *[Pause]* Look around. *[Pause]* Our group is together again. Welcome back!

Conclude the Meditation

Close the time of meditation with an appropriate prayer (for example, Glory Be to the Father) or a sung refrain (for example, Alleluia) that the children already know. You may wish to add easy-to-learn gestures.

Healed by Faith ⇾

Set the Stage

Prepare the children to enter into prayer by helping them reflect on their own experiences. Ask some leading questions. Use the questions below or questions of your own.

- Have you ever helped someone you didn't know? What did you do? Why?

- Have you ever met or heard about someone whom you think has a lot of faith? How could you tell?

Read the Scripture

Prepare the children to hear the Scripture by linking their experience to the Scripture theme. Use these words or your own.

> Let's listen to a story from the Gospel of Luke in which the servant of a Roman officer is healed by Jesus. Even though Jesus and the servant never actually meet, Jesus heals the servant because of the faith of the Roman officer.

Luke 7:1–10

> After Jesus had finished all his sayings in the hearing of the people, he entered Capernaum. A centurion there had a slave whom he valued highly, and who was ill and close to death. When he heard about Jesus, he sent some Jewish elders to him, asking him to come and heal his slave. When they came to Jesus, they appealed to him earnestly, saying, "He is worthy of having you do this for him, for he loves our people, and it is he who built our synagogue for us." And Jesus went with them, but when he was not far from the house, the centurion sent friends to say to him, "Lord, do not trouble yourself, for I am not worthy to have you come under my roof; therefore I did not presume to come to you. But only speak the word, and let my servant be healed. For I also am a man set under authority, with soldiers under me; and I say to one, 'Go, and he goes, and to another, 'Come,' and he comes, and to my slave, 'Do this,' and the

slave does it." When Jesus heard this he was amazed at him, and turning to the crowd that followed him, he said, "I tell you, not even in Israel have I found such faith." When those who had been sent returned to the house, they found the slave in good health.

Connect the Experience

Help the children connect their experience to the theme of the prayer. Use these words or your own.

Now we're going to use our imaginations and spend some time with Jesus. As you share with Jesus the Scripture you just heard, think of what this story tells us about our own relationship with Jesus.

Prepare for Prayer

First, invite the children to make themselves as comfortable as they can. Next, lead them to grow quiet by focusing on their breath.

To enter into this time of prayer, we first need to make ourselves comfortable. Leave enough space around you so that nothing distracts you. *[Pause]* Now close your eyes and let yourself grow still. *[Pause]* Take a few moments to pay attention to your breath. *[Pause]* Can you feel your breath make your chest rise and fall? *[Pause]* Take a slow, deep breath in *[Pause]*, hold *[Pause]*, then slowly and silently exhale. *[Pause]* Again, take another slow, deep breath in *[Pause]*, hold *[Pause]*, and silently exhale. *[Pause, and repeat as necessary]*

Lead the Meditation

Imagine yourself walking in your neighborhood on a sunny morning. *[Pause]* Look up to the sky. It's filled with clouds. Can you find any familiar shapes in them? That can be a fun thing to do. *[Pause]* Is there anyone else walking at this time of day? *[Pause]* Notice everyone around you. Bring your whole neighborhood into your imagination. *[Pause]*

As you walk, you feel safe and happy. Coming toward you is someone you know well. It's Jesus! He's come to be with you. You greet each other warmly. After saying hello, you and Jesus talk about what you will do next. Will you continue to walk? Or maybe you'd rather find a place to sit and talk. Make your decision together now. *[Pause]*

Jesus surprises you by bringing your favorite snack. What is it? Mmm. It tastes good. (*Pause*) You take your time eating, knowing that Jesus is not in a hurry. He wants to talk with you. Maybe Jesus asks what you were thinking about before he came along. Even if it was nothing, you can tell him that. It's even OK to just be together in silence for a while. *[Pause]*

Jesus continues the conversation by asking about the story you just heard. Think for a moment and tell him. He's eager to hear what you have to say. *[Pause]* Jesus wants to know if you'd like to talk about how he helped the Roman officer by curing his servant. Do you wonder why Jesus would help someone he'd never even seen or met? He's right here with you, so go ahead and ask him. *[Pause]*

What about you? Jesus wonders if you ever helped someone you'd never seen or met before. Tell him what you remember. *[Pause]* Maybe you and your friends made cards for someone in the parish who was sick. Or you might have collected canned foods for people who were hungry. Is there anything else you remember? Tell Jesus about it. *[Pause]*

Jesus recognized that the Roman officer was not asking for something for himself. The officer knew that Jesus had power that he himself didn't have. He believed that Jesus could cure his sick servant even without seeing him. You know that Jesus was very impressed with the Roman officer. Do you think that he was impressed with the Roman officer's concern for his sick servant? Was Jesus more impressed that someone as powerful as an officer in the Roman army would ask for help? Or was he impressed with something else? What do you think? *[Pause]*

Do you wonder if what impressed Jesus most of all was the Roman officer's faith? He had never seen Jesus. He had never met Jesus. He had only heard about him. Yet he believed in Jesus. *[Pause]* You can tell by the way Jesus is speaking that this is all very important. Ask him to help you see what God wants you to learn from this story. *[Pause]* Perhaps now you want to tell Jesus that you too believe in him. *[Pause]* If words don't come, that's OK. Jesus knows what's in your heart. Just sit quietly and open your heart to the unconditional love Jesus has for you. *[Long pause]*

Now Jesus has another question for you. He wants to know if you would like to go with him for a few minutes to be with God the Father. God loves spending time with you. *[Pause]*

And now for the best part! You and Jesus sit quietly together, heart-to-heart with God our Father. *[Pause]* Let yourself be loved by God. *[Pause]* Feel the great love God has for you. *[Pause]* With an open heart, just rest silently in God's presence. *[Long pause]* If there is something you would like to share with God, do it now. You know God loves to hear from you. *[Pause]* Listen for anything God might have to share with you. *[Pause]*

You sense it will soon be time to leave. You say goodbye for now to God the Father, and then you and Jesus go back to your neighborhood. *[Pause]* You thank Jesus for this time together, and before you leave, you ask Jesus to bless you. *[Pause]* You thank him for the gift of faith and ask him to help you become stronger in your faith. *[Pause]*

You and Jesus say goodbye for now. *[Pause]* You know you can spend time with him whenever you'd like. Gradually bring yourself back to this room. *[Pause]* Open your eyes. *[Pause]* Stretch if you'd like. *[Pause]* Look around. *[Pause]* Our group is together again. Welcome back!

Conclude the Meditation

Close the time of meditation with an appropriate prayer (for example, Glory Be to the Father) or a sung refrain (for example, Alleluia) which the children already know. You may wish to add easy-to-learn gestures.

I Hold You in My Heart ⤜

Set the Stage

Prepare the children to enter into prayer by helping them reflect on their own experiences. Ask some leading questions. Use the questions below or questions of your own.

- How can you tell when someone loves you?

- Have you ever tried to make someone happy even though it was difficult for you at the time? How did you do it?

Read the Scripture

Prepare the children to hear the Scripture by linking their experience to the Scripture theme. Use these words or your own.

> We're going to listen to a part of a letter that Saint Paul wrote to the Christians in Philippi. Even though he was in jail when he wrote the letter, his joy and gratitude to his friends in Philippi are strong and clear. He shares with them what is in his heart.

Philippians 1:3–11

> I thank my God every time I remember you, constantly praying with joy in every one of my prayers for all of you, because of your sharing in the gospel from the first day until now. I am confident of this, that the one who began a good work among you will bring it to completion by the day of Jesus Christ. It is right for me to think this way about all of you, because you hold me in your heart, for all of you share in God's grace with me, both in my imprisonment and in the defense and confirmation of the gospel. For God is my witness, how I long for all of you with the compassion of Christ Jesus. And this is my prayer, that your love may overflow more and more with knowledge and full insight to help you to determine what is best, so that in the day of Christ you may be pure and blameless, having produced the harvest of righteousness that comes through Jesus Christ for the glory and praise of God.

Connect the Experience

Help the children connect their experience to the theme of the prayer. Use the following words or your own.

> Now we're going to use our imaginations and spend some time with Jesus in a favorite quiet place. As you speak with him in prayer, remember the people you care about and hold in your heart.

Prepare for Prayer

First, invite the children to make themselves as comfortable as they can. Next, lead them to grow quiet by focusing on their breath.

> To enter into this time of prayer, we first need to make ourselves comfortable. Leave enough space around you so that nothing distracts you. *[Pause]* Now close your eyes and let yourself grow still. *[Pause]* Take a few moments to pay attention to your breath. *[Pause]* Can you feel your breath make your chest rise and fall? *[Pause]* Take a slow, deep breath in *[Pause]*, hold *[Pause]*, then slowly and silently exhale. *[Pause]* Again, take another slow, deep breath in *[Pause]*, hold *[Pause]*, and silently exhale *[Pause, and repeat as necessary]*

Lead the Meditation

> Where do you go when you need time to be quiet? *[Pause]* Do you have a special place? *[Pause]* Maybe you stay in bed and pull a blanket over your head. Or do you create a private place just by closing your eyes? *[Pause]* Wherever you go, imagine you are there now. *[Pause]* Invite Jesus to join you. He's the one person who's always welcome, isn't he? *[Pause]*
>
> Jesus is with you now. He's eager to listen and talk. Jesus always likes to hear what you have to say, so you can tell him what's on your mind. *[Pause]* Do you start by telling him about the ordinary things in your life: the pizza you had the other day, the latest movie you saw, or maybe the friend you spent time with? *[Pause]*
>
> Or maybe some more serious things are on your mind. Do you tell Jesus about the Scripture you just heard, the letter of Saint Paul's? You remember it's so full of love and joy. It's hard to believe that Paul wrote it from prison! Prison—not a pleasant place to be. Yet Paul stayed happy. How do you think that was possible for him? *[Pause]* You might want to ask Jesus about it. *[Pause]*

Does Jesus wonder if you heard this phrase in the Scripture: *"It is right for me to think this way about all of you, because you hold me in your heart . . ."* What a loving thing for Paul to say. Perhaps Jesus asks you whom it is that you hold in your heart. *[Pause]* Did anybody ever ask you a question like that before? Maybe you could think out loud with Jesus as you try to answer. Whom is it that you love? Who loves you? That's an easy way to start. Maybe you mention the people in your family first. *[Pause]* Who else? It's up to you to name anyone you'd like. Take your time. *[Pause]*

Jesus sits quietly with you while you do this. Does he say anything to you? *[Pause]* Now pick one or two of the people who love you very much. Your parents? Your grandparents? An aunt or uncle? You know who they are. Share their names with Jesus. *[Pause]* How do they show you that they love you? *[Pause]* Let Jesus know all the good things they do for you. *[Pause]*

Now Jesus has another question for you. In his letter, Saint Paul thanks God for many people. Besides the people you know and love, whom do you hold in your heart? *[Pause]* That's a much harder question, and maybe you're not sure yet how to answer. A good clue is to pay attention to the people you pray for. Who do you pray for at Mass, or at home, or in your heart? Can you answer that? *[Pause]* Maybe a relative who is sick, a friend who has a hard test coming up, a family that doesn't have enough to eat, a neighbor who has no job, or someone you saw on the street the other day. *[Pause]*

Perhaps you realize that there are many people to hold in your heart. Perhaps you wonder how you can love and care for them all. Jesus knows how. Ask him for help. *[Pause]* Jesus also knows how busy you might be. But nobody's too busy to glance at someone. So why not every so often during the day, give God in your heart a loving glance? *[Pause]* Then glance at all the people you hold in your heart. You and God can be together, looking at them and loving them. *[Pause]* Jesus asks if you'd like to do that now, spend time with God and open your heart to him. *[Pause]*

And now for the best part! You and Jesus sit quietly with God the Father, opening your heart and all of the people you hold there to God. *[Pause]* Just rest there in God's presence. Feel God's unconditional love for you and for all those you hold in your heart. *[Long pause]*

You sense that it will soon be time to go. You know you can return here whenever you want. You thank God for the gift of all those people who are special to you, all those people you hold in your heart. *[Pause]* Then you and Jesus return to your special quiet place. *[Pause]* As you turn to say goodbye to Jesus for now, you ask him to bless you and everyone you love. *[Pause]*

Gradually bring yourself back to this room. *[Pause]* Open your eyes. *[Pause]* Stretch if you'd like. *[Pause]* Look around. *[Pause]* Our group is together again. Welcome back!

Conclude the Meditation

Close the time of meditation with an appropriate prayer (for example, Glory Be to the Father) or a sung refrain (for example, Alleluia) that the children already know. You may wish to add easy-to-learn gestures.

I Am Always with You ⤳

Set the Stage

Prepare the children to enter into prayer by helping them reflect on their own experiences. Ask some leading questions. Use the questions below or questions of your own.

- Have you ever been given a big task to do and didn't know where to begin? What did you do?

- Did you ever have to go somewhere or do something that you didn't want to do alone? What did you do? How did it work out?

Read the Scripture

Prepare the children to hear the Scripture by linking their experience to the Scripture theme. Use these words or your own.

> Today we're going to hear a short section from the end of Matthew's Gospel. Jesus is risen and is giving instructions to his disciples before he ascends into heaven. He gives them a very big task to carry out in his name. He also makes them a very big promise.

> **Matthew 28:19–20**

> "Go therefore and make disciples of all nations, baptizing them in the name of the Father and of the Son and of the Holy Spirit, and teaching them to obey everything that I have commanded you. And remember, I am with you always, to the end of the age."

Connect the Experience

Help the children connect their experience to the theme of the prayer. Use the following words or your own.

> Now we're going to use our imaginations to go back in time to be with Jesus and the disciples in Galilee. As you join the disciples and observe them, open your heart to receive the message and the promise that Jesus offers.

Prepare for Prayer

First, invite the children to make themselves as comfortable as they can. Next, lead them to grow quiet by focusing on their breath.

> To enter into this time of prayer, we first need to make ourselves comfortable. Leave enough space around you so that nothing distracts you. *[Pause]* Now close your eyes and let yourself grow still. *[Pause]* Take a few moments to pay attention to your breath. *[Pause]* Can you feel your breath make your chest rise and fall? *[Pause]* Take a slow, deep breath in *[Pause]*, hold *[Pause]*, then slowly and silently exhale. *[Pause]* Again, take another slow, deep breath in *[Pause]*, hold *[Pause]*, and silently exhale. *[Pause, and repeat as necessary]*

Lead the Meditation

> Let's start out by imagining yourself in a faraway place, the place where Jesus lived, in the faraway time when he lived. *[Pause]* When you are there, imagine yourself among Jesus' first apostles. What do they look like? What are they doing? *[Pause]* Listen to them talking. *[Pause]* They know Jesus has been raised from the dead; some have even seen him. What are they saying to one another? *[Pause]* Be there quietly among them. Look around. *[Pause]* Jesus is there too. See him look at you, smile, and maybe even tell you he's glad you're there. How do you respond to him? *[Pause]*

> All the apostles are watching Jesus, so you do too. Jesus faces all of you. He looks very loving and very serious. As you look around, so does everyone else. This is an important meeting, and everyone seems to know it. *[Pause]* Jesus is telling all of you what he wants you to do. You listen very hard. You hear him say "Go, therefore, and make disciples of all nations . . ." What do you think about that? Does it surprise you? Go to *all* nations? How can you do that? *[Pause]*

> Now Jesus doesn't expect you to go to China, Russia, or Kenya. If people do whatever they can wherever they live, then Jesus' message will reach every nation. That doesn't sound quite so challenging, does it? Perhaps you think that this is a lot of food for thought, but Jesus has even more to say. Listen together with the apostles. *[Pause]* Jesus goes right on saying ". . . teaching them to obey everything that I have commanded you."

> What are the things he means when he says "everything that I have commanded you"? *[Pause]* Maybe you and the apostles can

talk this over. After all, they had Jesus himself teaching them for three years. What are some of the most important things Jesus said to do? *[Pause]* Maybe they're saying things such as "Love God with all your heart and soul, with all of yourself. Love one another as I have loved you." Do you remember anything else Jesus said to do? *[Pause]* Remember what Jesus did and how he treated people. He wants you to do the same with the people that you meet. Maybe you need some time to think about that. *[Pause]* What are some ways you will do this? What ideas do you have? *[Pause]*

Jesus has another very important thing to say: "And remember, I am with you always, to the end of the age." Listen to him with your heart wide open. Let his words fill your heart. *[Long pause]* Jesus is telling you that he is with you, always with you, every minute of every day, until the end of the world. Perhaps when you hear this, you feel yourself growing quiet inside. Do you sense that what Jesus is saying is terribly important for you and for everyone? *[Pause]* Maybe you need some time to let it all sink in.

Perhaps you look around for a quiet place nearby where no one is likely to notice you. When you are there, go down deep into your heart to that place where God and you can meet. *[Pause]* Share with God the Father what you just heard Jesus say. *[Pause]* Ask God about it if you want. Or tell God what you think. Or just be quiet with God, letting your heart and mind be filled with this great, good truth: I am with you always. *[Long pause]*

You sense that it is time to return to Jesus and the apostles. Thank God the Father for this time together and then make your way back over to the group. *[Pause]* Maybe you still are wondering about what Jesus meant when he talked about making disciples of all nations. Now this is probably something you still need to think about further, what it means to you personally. But you just heard Jesus say that he is with you always. You can always turn to him for advice. Maybe you'd like to do that now. He loves spending time with you and listening to your thoughts and questions. What advice would you like to ask of Jesus? *[Pause]*

You sense it will soon be time to return to the room. You thank Jesus for being with us all of the time. Maybe you want to ask him to remind you of that every so often. *[Pause]* If there's anything else you'd like to say to Jesus, take a moment now to do so. *[Pause]* You say goodbye to Jesus for now and wave to each other as you leave.

When you are ready, gradually come back to the room. *[Pause]* Open your eyes. *[Pause]* Stretch if you'd like. *[Pause]* Look around. *[Pause]* See our group and know that we're back together.

Conclude the Meditation

Close the time of meditation with an appropriate prayer (such as, Glory Be to the Father) or a sung refrain (such as, Alleluia) that the children already know. You may wish to add easy-to-learn gestures.

The Vine and the Branches ⇥

Set the Stage

Prepare the children to enter into prayer by helping them reflect on their own experiences. Ask some leading questions. Use the questions below or questions of your own.

- Have you ever seen grapes grow? What does a vineyard look like?

- How do you stay in touch with relatives and friends that live far away?

Read the Scripture

Prepare the children to hear the Scripture by linking their experience to the Scripture theme. Use these words or your own.

> Today we're going to hear a section from John's Gospel. Jesus compares himself to a grapevine and says that we are like the branches. Our job is to be fruitful. Then Jesus tells us how to accomplish that.

John 15:1–5

> "I am the true vine, and my Father is the vinegrower. He removes every branch in me that bears no fruit. Every branch that bears fruit he prunes to make it bear more fruit. You have already been cleansed by the word that I have spoken to you. Abide in me as I abide in you. Just as the branch cannot bear fruit by itself unless it abides in the vine, neither can you unless you abide in me. I am the vine, you are the branches. Those who abide in me and I in them bear much fruit, because apart from me you can do nothing."

Connect the Experience

Help the children connect their experience to the theme of the prayer. Use these words or your own.

Today we're going to use our imaginations to go back in time and be with Jesus in the land where he lived. Even though you've never been there, anything is possible in our imaginations. As you walk with Jesus through the vineyards, think about the ways you stay connected to God.

Prepare for Prayer

First, invite the children to make themselves as comfortable as they can. Next, lead them to grow quiet by focusing on their breath.

To enter into this time of prayer, we first need to make ourselves comfortable. Leave enough space around you so that nothing distracts you. *[Pause]* Now close your eyes and let yourself grow still. *[Pause]* Take a few moments to pay attention to your breath. *[Pause]* Can you feel your breath make your chest rise and fall? *[Pause]* Take a slow, deep breath in *[Pause]*, hold *[Pause]*, then slowly and silently exhale. *[Pause]* Again, take another slow, deep breath in *[Pause]*, hold *[Pause]*, and silently exhale *[Pause, and repeat as necessary]*

Lead the Meditation

Imagine that you're in Galilee at the time when Jesus lived. *[Pause]* As you look around, you realize that you are seeing some of the very things that Jesus saw every day. *[Pause]* What do you think this land that was home to Jesus looked like? Was it flat or hilly? Was it sunny or cloudy? Hot or cold? Picture it in your mind. *[Pause]*

One thing we know for certain is that there were many vineyards in the area, places where bunches of grapes grow on thick vines in long rows. Green grapes, purple grapes, red grapes. Round and juicy. You're invited to try some. How do they taste? Would you like to try some more? *[Pause]* Jesus knew vineyards well and even used them in his parables, the stories that he used to teach the people.

Imagine that Jesus walks toward you and asks you to take a walk with him through a vineyard. You laugh because you figure Jesus knows you just heard the parable of the vine and the branches. Do you tell him that? Does Jesus laugh too? *[Pause]* If you have questions about this story but are too embarrassed to ask, don't be. Jesus is a teacher. And that's what teachers do—explain things. So you ask what he means when he says "I am the vine and you are the branches." *[Pause]*

Jesus might ask you what would happen if one of the branches broke off the vine. Think about that for a minute. Have you ever seen what happens when a branch breaks off? *[Pause]* Jesus wants you to know that this story has to do with staying connected. Think about it. Do you have any friends who live far away? Do your cousins or grandparents live in another state? How do you keep in touch with people who are far away? *[Pause]* Do you phone them, e-mail them, write letters? *[Pause]* If you don't stay connected some way, what happens? *[Pause]* Sometimes you can forget about people, or they begin to forget about you. It can take extra time to stay connected.

It's the same way with Jesus. We need to stay connected with him. We need his help, his grace. He gives it to us. That's his part. Our part is to pray. Our prayer is like our e-mail, our phone call, our letter to Jesus. *[Pause]* Do you set aside a special time to pray? *[Pause]* Maybe you'd like to start now. What is a good time for you? Is it when you get out of bed in the morning? After dinner? Before you go to sleep? *[Pause]*

Why not take some time now to talk with Jesus? He's right here with you. And even though he knows everything about you all the time, he likes to hear from you about the things that are going on in your life. Talk to him. Tell him the good and the not so good. *[Long pause]* Then listen. You will find his message in your heart. *[Pause]*

Now Jesus has a question for you. He wants to know if you would like to go with him for a few minutes to be with God the Father. God loves spending time with you. *[Pause]*

And now for the best part! You and Jesus sit quietly together, heart-to-heart with God our Father. *[Pause]* Let yourself be loved by God. *[Pause]* Feel the great love God has for you. *[Pause]* With an open heart, just rest silently in God's presence. *[Long pause]* If there is something you would like to share with God, do it now. You know God loves to hear from you. *[Pause]* Listen for anything God might have to share with you. *[Pause]*

You sense that it's getting to be time to go. You know you can return here whenever you want. You thank God for Jesus and for being connected to him like grapes on a vine. Then you and Jesus return to the vineyard. *[Pause]*

Knowing that it's almost time to go back to the room, you thank Jesus for the story of the vine and the branches. Maybe you tell him that it will remind you to stay connected. You thank Jesus for teaching you through stories. Tell him how much you enjoyed this time together. And then you say goodbye for now. It's time to go.

Gradually come back to this room. *[Pause]* When you're ready, open your eyes. *[Pause]* Stretch if you'd like. *[Pause]* Look around. *[Pause]* See our group and know that we're back together.

Conclude the Meditation

Close the time of meditation with an appropriate prayer (for example, Glory Be to the Father) or a sung refrain (for example, Alleluia) that the children already know. You may wish to add easy-to-learn gestures.

Growing in Holiness ⇁

Set the Stage

Prepare the children to enter into prayer by helping them reflect on their own experiences. Ask some leading questions. Use the questions below or questions of your own.

- What do you think are some Godlike qualities?

- Have you ever met someone that you thought was holy? What was that person like?

Read the Scripture

Prepare the children to hear the Scripture by linking their experience to the Scripture theme. Use these words or your own.

> We're going to listen to a very short Scripture passage. It's only one sentence long. In this one sentence, God gives us a mission to live out one day at a time for our whole lives.

Leviticus 11:44

> For I am the LORD your God; sanctify yourselves therefore, and be holy, for I am holy.

Connect the Experience

Help the children connect their experience to the theme of the prayer. Use the following words or your own.

> Today we're going to use the gift of our imagination to go to our inner, quiet place and spend some time alone with Jesus. As you meet him in prayer, you might want to ask for the grace to see yourself as he sees you—as a loved and gifted child of God.

Prepare for Prayer

First, invite the children to make themselves as comfortable as they can. Next, lead them to grow quiet by focusing on their breath.

To enter into this time of prayer, we first need to make ourselves comfortable. Leave enough space around you so that nothing distracts you. *[Pause]* Now close your eyes and let yourself grow still. *[Pause]* Take a few moments to pay attention to your breath. *[Pause]* Can you feel your breath make your chest rise and fall? *[Pause]* Take a slow, deep breath in *[Pause]*, hold *[Pause]*, then slowly and silently exhale. *[Pause]* Again, take another slow, deep breath in *[Pause]*, hold *[Pause]*, and silently exhale *[Pause, and repeat as necessary]*

Lead the Meditation

Imagine yourself in a place where you'd like to be. It doesn't matter if you've never actually been there before. Imagine the way you think it looks. Maybe it's a place where you've met Jesus before; maybe it's a different one. You choose, because anything is possible in our imagination. *[Pause]* You can make it your favorite season of the year. *[Pause]* You can make the weather just the way you like it. *[Pause]* Just be there and look around and enjoy what you see and hear. *[Pause]*

Jesus comes to join you almost right away. He knew exactly where to find you. As he comes in sight, you go to meet him. He's obviously glad to see you. Do you wave? How do you greet each other? *[Pause]* Hear him tell you how glad he is to be with you again. *[Pause]*

As usual, Jesus asks you what you've been doing. Sometimes your answer to that question would be "Not much." But today it's different. He asks you about the Scripture verse you just heard: "For I am the Lord your God; sanctify yourselves therefore, and be holy, for I am holy." Now that's not your usual line of thought. But there's something in this verse that puzzles you. You probably don't have trouble with the idea of God being holy. But the idea of you being holy, of making and keeping yourself holy, what do you think about that? Perhaps it needs a little more explanation. Let Jesus know what you're thinking. *[Pause]*

Now Jesus has a question for you. He asks you to think of qualities that you would use to describe God—maybe qualities such as loving, forgiving, patient, understanding and generous. What else would you add to this list? *[Pause]* Let's call all of these "God qualities." Then Jesus might ask you to think of someone you know who has some of these God qualities. You might need to think for a minute. Who is it? Share with Jesus why you chose this person. *[Pause]*

Jesus, a great storyteller himself, might ask you to share a story about this person, something that demonstrates the God qualities that this person has. It may take some time to choose just one story, but that's OK. Take the time to remember and then share something of this person with Jesus. *[Pause]* Maybe this one story makes you remember other stories. Take your time and share those memories with Jesus. *[Pause]*

Perhaps Jesus reminds you that God is all-holy. Jesus might tell you that you are holy when you act in a Godlike manner. When you live your life with generosity, understanding and patience, then you are holy. Yes, *you*! You are holy. What an awesome statement! And it is true! Maybe you want to think about that for a minute. *[Pause]* Maybe you tell Jesus that being holy is what you want, but sometimes you feel unable to live up to that calling. *[Pause]*

As usual, Jesus is reassuring. He wants you to know that you don't become holy all at once. You grow in holiness. You'll make mistakes just like everyone does, but that's OK. You can always learn from them. Each day you wake up and try again. Perhaps Jesus reminds you that the Holy Spirit is always with you to guide you. Jesus says that he himself will help you anytime you need him. *[Pause]* How does that make you feel? *[Pause]*

Go with Jesus now deep down into your heart. You've shared a lot with him already, so now just rest in his love. There's no need for more words. Simply be still in each other's company. Feel the love and care that Jesus has for you. *[Long pause]*

Now Jesus turns to you and asks you a question. He wonders if you would like to go with him for a few minutes to be with God the Father. God loves being with you. *[Pause]*

And now for the best part! You and Jesus sit quietly together, heart-to-heart with God our Father. *[Pause]* Let yourself be loved by God. Feel the great love God has for you. *[Pause]* With an open heart, just rest in God's presence. *[Long pause]* If there is something you would like to share with God, do it now. You know God loves to hear from you. *[Pause]* Listen for anything God might have to share with you. *[Pause]*

You sense that it will soon be time to leave. You know you can return here whenever you want. You thank God for this time together. Then you and Jesus return to your special place. *[Pause]* As you turn to say goodbye, you ask him to help you grow in holiness. *[Pause]* Take a moment to tell Jesus how much you enjoyed this time together. *[Pause] You say goodbye for now, knowing you can spend time with Jesus whenever you like. [Pause]*

Gradually bring yourself back to this room. *[Pause]* Open your eyes. *[Pause]* Stretch. *[Pause]* Look all around you. *[Pause]* Everyone's here. We're all back.

Conclude the Meditation

Close the time of meditation with an appropriate prayer (such as, Glory Be to the Father) or a sung refrain (such as, Alleluia) that the children already know. You may wish to add easy-to-learn gestures.

God is With Us ⤳

Set the Stage

Prepare the children to enter into prayer by helping them reflect on their own experiences. Ask some leading questions. Use the questions below or questions of your own.

- Have you ever had a dream that seemed real? How could you tell the difference?

- Do you know how you got your name? Do you know what your name means?

Read the Scripture

Prepare the children to hear the Scripture by linking their experience to the Scripture theme. Use these words or your own.

> We're going to listen to a story from Matthew's Gospel about the birth of Jesus. You've probably heard it many times. This time, listen carefully to what the angel tells Joseph to do.

Matthew 1:18–24

> Now the birth of Jesus the Messiah took place in this way. When his mother Mary had been engaged to Joseph, but before they lived together, she was found to be with child from the Holy Spirit. Her husband Joseph, being a righteous man and unwilling to expose her to public disgrace, planned to dismiss her quietly. But just when he had resolved to do this, an angel of the Lord appeared to him in a dream and said, "Joseph, son of David, do not be afraid to take Mary as your wife, for the child conceived in her is from the Holy Spirit. She will bear a son, and you are to name him Jesus, for he will save his people from their sins." All this took place to fulfill what had been spoken by the Lord through the prophet:
>
>> "Look, the virgin shall conceive and bear a son,
>> And they shall name him Emmanuel,"

which means, "God is with us." When Joseph awoke from sleep, he did as the angel of the Lord commanded him.

Connect the Experience

Help the children connect their experience to the theme of the prayer. Use these words or your own.

> Today we're going to use our imaginations and let a ball of red string lead us back to Bethlehem at the time when Jesus was born. As you enter the stable where Mary, Joseph, and the baby Jesus are, let yourself be open to the miracle of God taking on human flesh and being born as a baby.

Prepare for Prayer

First, invite the children to make themselves as comfortable as they can. Next, lead them to grow quiet by focusing on their breath.

> To enter into this time of prayer, we first need to make ourselves comfortable. Leave enough space around you so that nothing distracts you. *[Pause]* Now close your eyes and let yourself grow still. *[Pause]* Take a few moments to pay attention to your breath. *[Pause]* Can you feel your breath make your chest rise and fall? *[Pause]* Take a slow, deep breath in *[Pause]*, hold *[Pause]*, then slowly and silently exhale. *[Pause]* Again, take another slow, deep breath in *[Pause]*, hold *[Pause]*, and silently exhale. *[Pause, and repeat as necessary]*

Lead the Meditation

> Imagine that you're walking in an open field next to a forest. The weather is just how you like it. Do you feel a breeze? Is it warm or cool? As you walk, you feel happy. You're going to your Heart Home, that place deep inside you where you can talk with Jesus. You're walking along, and you see an old woman sitting on a rock. She's smiling. You know somehow that you've seen her before, and you can tell that she's kind. "Are you looking for your Heart Home?" she asks. "Yes," you answer. "Here, catch!" says the woman as she tosses you a big ball of red string. Then she says "If you want to find your Heart Home, hold the ball of red string in front of your heart." *[Pause]*

> You hold the ball of red string just as she says and repeat the words that she tells you to say: "Red string, red string, I will follow you, my red string. Red string, red string, take me to my

Heart Home." *[Pause]* Then she tells you to toss the string out in front of you and follow it. You throw it, and the ball of red string starts to roll away into the forest. You follow it. At first, the string rolls slowly by some tall trees. It passes the trees and stops in a clearing of wildflowers. Can you smell them? Aren't the colors brilliant? *[Pause]*

You look up and watch as the ball of red string magically weaves itself into a one-person airplane—just the right size for you. You climb inside. It's a perfect fit. You notice gauges and knobs and levers all around you. You're not quite sure what to do. See that green button labeled *start*? Push the button. What do you hear? *[Pause]* The power gathers and you see a blinking light. It says *Bethlehem.* Another light starts to blink. It says *A Long Time Ago.* Your airplane takes off. *[Pause]*

As you look out the window, you see amazing things—lakes and cities, mountains and deserts. What else do you see down below? *[Pause]* It's a quick flight, and now it's time to land. Your airplane makes a smooth landing and comes to a stop. You turn off the engine with a push of the *stop* button and climb outside into the night. *[Pause]*

As you look around, you see a flock of sheep. The sheep are grazing quietly. You notice the shepherds are nearby. Then you look up and see a very bright star in the sky. This must be near Bethlehem! Right before your very eyes the string airplane unravels and becomes a ball again. It rolls over to the shepherds, unwinding a little at a time. You ask the shepherds if they know about a stable where you could find a baby and his parents. *[Pause]* They smile and point in the direction of the star's light. The ball of string rolls in that direction and you follow it. *[Pause]*

What are you feeling as you follow the string to the stable? Quiet and peaceful? Or maybe excited? *[Pause]* You see the soft light of the glowing lamps inside. When you go in, you see Mary and Joseph and the baby. They notice you too, of course! They smile and introduce themselves. But you already knew who they were, didn't you? *[Pause]*

Mary looks down at the baby and tells you his name is Jesus. She might ask you what you've learned about him. Do you tell her that you know he is God's Son? Do you mention that he is a special gift to the world? Take some time to tell Mary what you know. *[Long pause]*

Mary is smiling at you so lovingly that you have the courage to ask if you could hold the baby. Mary smiles and comes closer. She knows you will be careful. You hold out your arms to receive Jesus. She gives him to you, ever so gently. *[Pause]* You look at him. His eyes are wide open, and he looks up at you and smiles. What do you do? Do you cuddle him? *[Pause]* Maybe you rock him or sing to him. *[Pause]* You decide and do it. *[Pause]*

Joseph shows you how to prop the baby against your left shoulder and pat his back softly. As you hold him you realize that his little heart is beating right against your heart! Instead of using words, let your heart love him and let his heart love you. *[Pause]* Feel what it's like to have your heart beat in rhythm with the Son of God. *[Long pause]*

You sense that the time is coming when you will need to leave. Who takes the baby from you, Mary or Joseph? *[Pause]* Together they thank you for coming and for being so gentle with their infant Son. You thank them for letting you join them at this time and hold him. Then you say goodbye to one another for now. *[Pause]*

At the door of the stable, you notice the curly end of the red string. As you walk toward it, the string begins to rewind. You follow it. *[Pause]* Just as before, the string weaves itself into an airplane. You climb inside and push the *start* button. The power gathers. You're on your way back.

You fly across the world and time, landing smoothly in the clearing of wildflowers. You climb out and watch as the string airplane becomes a ball of red string once more. The ball of string leads you through the flowers, past the trees, and back to where you started. *[Pause]*

Now slowly come back to this room. Open your eyes. *[Pause]* Stretch your arms and legs. *[Pause]* Notice your friends are all around you. *[Pause]* Welcome back!

Conclude the Meditation

Close the time of meditation with an appropriate prayer (such as, Glory Be to the Father) or a sung refrain (such as, Alleluia) that the children already know. You may wish to add easy-to-learn gestures.

Made in God's Image →

Set the Stage

Prepare the children to enter into prayer by helping them reflect on their own experiences. Ask some leading questions. Use the questions below or questions of your own.

- Have you ever made anything from scratch? What did you do? How did you do it?

- Do you know any identical twins? How do you tell them apart?

Read the Scripture

Prepare the children to hear the Scripture by linking their experience to the Scripture theme. Use these words or your own.

> We're going to listen to a story that will be very familiar to you. It's the story of how God created human beings in his own image and likeness. This privilege comes with responsibilities and is given with great love.

Genesis 1:26–31

> Then God said, "Let us make humankind in our image, according to our likeness; and let them have dominion over the fish of the sea, and over the birds of the air, and over the cattle, and over all the wild animals of the earth, and over every creeping thing that creeps upon the earth."
>
> > So God created humankind in his image,
> > in the image of God he created them;
> > male and female he created them.
>
> God blessed them, and God said to them, "Be fruitful and multiply, and fill the earth and subdue it; and have dominion over the fish of the sea and over the birds of the air and over every living thing that moves upon the earth." God said, "See, I have given you every plant yielding seed that is upon the face of all the earth, and every tree with seed in its fruit; you shall have them for food. And to every beast of the earth, and to every bird of the air, and to

everything that creeps on the earth, everything that has the breath of life, I have given every green plant for food." And it was so. God saw everything that he had made, and indeed, it was very good. And there was evening and there was morning, the sixth day.

Connect the Experience

Help the children connect their experience to the theme of the prayer. Use the following words or your own.

Today we're going to use our imaginations and let a ball of red string lead us inside ourselves where we can be alone with Jesus in prayer. As you share with him about the Scripture passage, listen carefully for all he wants to tell you about the gifts God created you with and how much God loves you.

Prepare for Prayer

First, invite the children to make themselves as comfortable as they can. Next, lead them to grow quiet by focusing on their breath.

To enter into this time of prayer, we first need to make ourselves comfortable. Leave enough space around you so that nothing distracts you. *[Pause]* Now close your eyes and let yourself grow still. *[Pause]* Take a few moments to pay attention to your breath. *[Pause]* Can you feel your breath make your chest rise and fall? *[Pause]* Take a slow, deep breath in *[Pause]*, hold *[Pause]*, then slowly and silently exhale. *[Pause]* Again, take another slow, deep breath in *[Pause]*, hold *[Pause]*, and silently exhale. *[Pause, and repeat as necessary]*

Lead the Meditation

Imagine that you are walking in a park next to a forest. The weather is just the way you like it. Is it warm or cool? *[Pause]* Do you feel a breeze? *[Pause]* You're on your way to a special place. You're going to your Heart Home, that place deep inside you where you can talk with Jesus. *[Pause]*

As you walk, you see an old woman sitting on a large rock. She sees you and smiles. You know somehow that you've seen her before, and you can tell that she's kind. "Are you looking for your Heart Home?" she asks. "Yes," you answer. "Here, catch!" says the woman as she tosses you a big ball of red string. Then she says "If you want to find your Heart Home, hold the ball of red string in front of your heart."

You hold the ball of red string just as she says and repeat the words that she tells you to say: "Red string, red string, I will follow you, my red string. Red string, red string, take me to my Heart Home." *[Pause]* Then she tells you to toss the string out in front of you and follow it. You throw it, and the ball of red string starts to roll off through the park.

At first, the string rolls slowly by a picnic table. The ball continues. It leads you into a grassy area. You're so intent you nearly miss the deer feeding over by the playground. Stop. Be very still as you watch them. *[Pause]* As they scatter through the park, follow the red string to the river. The river is too wide to cross by yourself. But the red string is there to help you. Watch. It does something special to help you get across without getting wet. What does the red string do? *[Pause]*

On the other side of the river is the forest. As you enter it, you notice that the ball of red string is getting very small. You continue to follow it. Now only the curly end of the string is left, reaching up from the ground. You've made it to your Heart Home! Jesus, your friend, welcomes you and asks you how things have been going. Tell him about your good days, bad days, and even the ones that are just so-so. *[Pause]*

Jesus is interested and listens without hurrying you. Then out of the blue, he asks if you know who created you. Well, of course, you know. You've known since you were little that God created you. Without explaining, Jesus reminds you that he was a carpenter. You know that too. He may go on telling you that when a carpenter makes a table and sells it, he might never have anything to do with it again. Does Jesus ask if this is how it is with God and you? Hmm. What do you think? Maybe you have an idea of where this is going. Maybe you don't have a clue. Whichever is true for you, tell Jesus. *[Pause]*

Jesus wants you to know that God is not like a carpenter. God did not create you and then leave you alone. God is with you every second of your life. No matter what happens—even if you forget or mess up—God is with you, loving you, helping you every single second of your existence. That is awesome! *[Pause]* God did not abandon Adam and Eve when he sent them out of the Garden, and he won't abandon you either, ever! Even if you abandon God, God will never abandon you. Take some more time with Jesus, mulling this over in your head and heart. *[Pause]*

You can tell by how Jesus is looking at you now that he has something very important to say, and so you listen with your whole heart. Jesus reminds you that when God made you, he made you with all the gifts and possibilities you have. Think of all the things that you can do now that you couldn't do when you were a baby. *[Pause]* You've come a long way, haven't you? Now try to imagine all the things you will be able to do as you continue to grow—things such as driving a car, going to college, and raising a family. Spend some time thinking about this with Jesus. *[Pause]*

Now Jesus turns to you and asks you a question. He wonders if you would like to go with him for a few minutes to be with God the Father. God loves spending time with you. *[Pause]*

And now for the best part! You and Jesus sit quietly together, heart-to-heart with God our Father. *[Pause]* Let yourself be loved by God. *[Pause]* With an open heart, just rest silently in God's presence. *[Long pause]* You know God loves to hear from you. *[Pause]* Listen for anything God might have to share with you. *[Pause]*

You sense that it will soon be time to leave. You know you can return here whenever you want. You thank God for this time together, and then you and Jesus turn to leave. Your time with Jesus is nearing the end, so take a moment to ask Jesus for his blessing and for whatever you most need right now. *[Pause]*

Say goodbye to Jesus for now, knowing that you will look forward to your next visit. Jesus walks with you back to the curly end of the red string. You nudge it with your toe and follow it back to the river. Once again, the red string helps you get across. *[Pause]* You walk back through the park to the place where you began. Then you put the rewound ball of red string into your imaginary pocket and bring your attention back to the present. *[Pause]*

Gradually bring yourself back to this room. *[Pause]* When you're ready, open your eyes. *[Pause]* Stretch. *[Pause]* Look around. *[Pause]* See the rest of our group. We're all back now.

Conclude the Meditation

Close the time of meditation with an appropriate prayer (such as, Glory Be to the Father) or a sung refrain (such as, Alleluia) which the children already know. You may wish to add easy-to-learn gestures.

Scripture Index